New
Ways

Story by Dawn McMillan

Illustrated by Meredith Thomas

Rigby PM Plus Chapter Books
part of the Rigby PM Program
Emerald Level

U.S. edition © 2003 Rigby Education
Harcourt Achieve Inc.
10801 N. MoPac Expressway
Building #3
Austin, TX 78759
www.harcourtachieve.com

Text © 2003 Thomson Learning Australia
Illustrations © 2003 Thomson Learning Australia
Originally published in Australia by Thomson Learning Australia

10 9 8 7 6 5
07

New Ways
   ISBN 0 7578 4116 3

Printed in China by 1010 Printing International Ltd.

Contents

Chapter 1

Waiting for Dad

Tess and Nathan sat on the window seat and looked out at the storm. The trees bent with the wind, and the rain beat against the glass. Tess watched the raindrops run down the pane and thought that they looked like tears. She looked at her watch. Dad was late!

Several times, Nathan jumped up expecting to see the blue truck turn into the drive, only to sit down again, disappointed. "Perhaps Dad's not coming," he muttered. "Perhaps we don't matter any more."

"Of course he's coming!" Tess snapped. "He promised, didn't he? And Grandma's expecting us too."

Mom came over to the window seat. "Dad will be here soon," she reassured them. "There'll be a good reason for him being late. He'd never let you down," she said quietly.

Just then the truck pulled up in front of the house.

"Here he is!" shouted Nathan as he grabbed his coat and backpack and raced to the front door. "See you tomorrow, Mom!" he called over his shoulder.

Tess picked up her jacket and followed him. "Will you be all right, Mom?" she asked.

Mom laughed, just a little too loudly.
"I'll be fine. It'll be great to have some
peace and quiet!"

Tess raced back to give Mom a hug.
"You'll miss us!" she teased. "We love
you," she whispered, then she put her
jacket on and ran out into the rain.

Chapter 2

A Right Time to Cry

"Hi, Dad! You're late!" exclaimed Nathan as he slipped into the back seat of the truck and twisted out of his wet coat.

Tess opened the front door and jumped in out of the rain. "We were worried," she said.

Dad grinned. "So was I!" he said. "I thought I'd never get here! There was a tree down across River Road. I had to take a detour."

Dad backed the truck down the drive. Nathan and Tess waved to Mom as they drove away down the street.

"I hope Mom will be okay," whispered Nathan.

Dad nodded his head. "So do I," he said quietly.

There was a moment of silence, then Dad spoke up. "Your Grandma has a big pot of homemade soup on the stove. She'll be wondering where we are."

Tess thought of how much Mom loved homemade soup. *It's not fair,* she thought. *This whole separation thing isn't fair!* She felt the tears pushing against her eyelids. She blinked hard and turned her face to the window. She couldn't cry now. She'd upset Dad, and Grandma would see her red eyes. *There's never a right time to cry,* she thought.

Dad's voice cut into her thoughts. "Are you all right, Tess?" he asked, as he touched her arm.

Tess nodded. "I'm fine," she said.

"You don't look fine to me," Nathan said. "You're going to cry!"

"I am not!" Tess shouted.

Dad slowed down and pulled the truck over. "I'm sorry," he whispered. "I don't want you two to be sad."

Tess felt her breath catch. A tear escaped and rolled down her cheek.

"Hey, it's okay to cry," Dad said gently. "I've got some tissues here somewhere," he said, opening the glove box. "I need them myself sometimes!"

Nathan watched Tess wipe her face. He felt a hard lump in his chest, and his face burned as Dad reached over and squeezed his shoulder. "Let's go, Dad," he said. "Grandma will be getting worried about us."

Dad nodded, and drove off again. "It'll get easier with time," he promised. "Easier for all of us."

Chapter 3

Jigsaw Pieces

Grandma opened the door and helped Tess and Nathan hang up their coats. They could feel the heat from the fire, and a delicious smell wafted from the kitchen.

"Go and dry off," she said. "I'll serve the lunch. You must be starving! I thought you'd never get here!"

Tess and Nathan sat on the rug and held their hands up in front of the fire, while Dad told Grandma about the tree. Then Grandma brought a tray to the table, loaded with a plate of toast and four steaming bowls of homemade soup.

"Here you are," she said.

"Yum!" grinned Dad. "My favorite!"

"Just as well you have Grandma to look after you, Dad," Nathan said, as he chewed his toast.

Dad nodded and put his spoon down. "I am lucky," he said. "But I do need to get my own place. Remember, you two are going to help me find a house."

Nathan put his spoon down. Suddenly he wasn't hungry any more. "You could come home to our house," he said. "Then you wouldn't need to buy another one."

"I can't do that, Nathan," Dad answered.

"We'll help you with your house, Dad," Tess said quietly. "Remember, Nathan. We promised."

"Good," Dad sighed. "If the rain stops, we can make a start tomorrow. It'll be fun."

"Eat your soup," Grandma said. "And then you can help me! I've got a jigsaw puzzle out with 1000 pieces, and I've only managed to do the corners!"

After lunch Dad snoozed in the chair while Tess, Nathan, and Grandma worked on the puzzle.

"I hate our family being separated!" Nathan said angrily. "Why can't we all live together?"

Grandma picked up a puzzle piece. "Sometimes families are like puzzles," she said thoughtfully. "No matter how hard you try, the pieces just don't seem to fit together. Just wait a while, Nathan. It will get better. You'll get used to the new ways of being a family."

"That's what Dad said," Tess said quietly.

Then Nathan started to cry. "But it'll never be as good as it was. We'll never be a proper family again," he sobbed.

"Be patient, Nathan," said Grandma as she gave him a hug.

Chapter 4

House-hunting

The next morning the sun was shining. Nathan woke first. He jumped from his bed and ran down the hall to Tess's room.

"Wake up, Tess!" he called. "It's stopped raining. We're going house-hunting!"

Tess pulled the blankets up to her ears. She could hear the excitement in Nathan's voice. "If Dad buys a house, then there's *no* chance of him coming home again!" she said to herself.

She pushed the blankets back and walked to the window. Nathan was right. The sun was shining and the wind had dropped.

Tess dressed and made her way downstairs. Dad and Nathan were eating breakfast.

"Grandma's sleeping late this morning," Dad said. "We can slip out quietly and see which places catch the morning sun in the winter. What do you think, Tess?"

Tess sat down. "Good idea," she said quietly.

"Eat your breakfast first," Dad laughed. "We can't go without breakfast when we have such an important job to do!"

Tess looked at Dad. He seemed happy about finding a new house. She felt a stir of anger deep down inside. She wanted to ask him why he was so happy about living separately, but she poured the milk on her cereal and said nothing.

All morning Dad and Tess and Nathan drove around looking at houses, but nothing they saw looked right. Then suddenly Tess saw a small house tucked in among some tall trees, right at the end of a dead-end street.

"Look, Dad," she pointed. "That one's for sale!"

Dad drove down the street and pulled up alongside the house. The trees spread their branches over the fence, as if to invite them in.

"I could make a treehouse in that big tree!" said Nathan excitedly.

Dad sat and looked at the house. "I like this one," he said at last.

They all climbed out of the truck and stood on the sidewalk.

"It needs some paint," Dad said. "And the yard could do with some work. But I like it!"

Tess drew in her breath. Dad was going to buy this house, she could tell. She liked the house, too. And so did Nathan.

"I don't want you to live away from us, Dad," she said softly. "If you buy this house you'll never come home. Can't you and Mom be together again?"

Dad spoke gently. "I'm not coming back, Tess. Mom and I are both sure that we'll stay separated."

"Why can't you sort it out?" Nathan shouted. "What's wrong with you two anyway?"

Chapter 5

A Long Story

Dad put his arms around them both and led them to the truck.

"Your mom and I tried so hard to stay together," Dad said. "We even saw a counselor."

"What's a counselor?" interrupted Nathan.

"Someone who helps people solve their problems," Tess answered, feeling important.

"Well, it didn't work!" Nathan snapped, the tears stinging his eyes.

"No," Dad agreed.

"What went wrong, Dad?" Tess asked.

Dad sighed. "It's a long story, Tess," he said. "We were so happy to begin with, and we were so proud when you two came along."

"Then it's our fault!" Nathan sobbed. "We changed things."

"No, Nathan!" cried Dad. "It could never be your fault. You're wonderful children. No, we just started to drift apart. We started liking different things, and thinking in different ways. It just happened, and we're both really sorry."

"You don't love each other any more?" Nathan asked.

Dad replied, "Your mom and I will always be friends, but being married needs a different kind of love."

Tess turned to Nathan and said quietly, "It'll be all right, Nathan. We'll get used to it. We've still got our mom and our dad. And it'll be fun coming to this house."

Chapter 6

One Thing Never Changes

When Dad took Tess and Nathan home, Mom was working in the garden. She stood up and took off her gloves.

"Hello, you two," she said as they climbed out of the truck. "Have you had a good time?"

"We helped Dad find a house," said Nathan proudly. "He's going to help me make a treehouse!" he added.

"We're going to help Dad with the painting, and the garden," Tess said.

Mom laughed. "You two are both talking at once!" she said. "I can see that you are going to enjoy helping your dad."

"We'll help you too," said Tess quickly. "We can clear some of these weeds."

"Thanks, Tess," Mom said. "Why don't you go and butter some muffins. Dad and I'll be in soon. We just need to have a little chat."

Tess and Nathan raced inside.

"It's good to be home," said Nathan.

Tess laughed. "We're going to have two homes now," she said.

Mom and Dad came into the kitchen and Dad sat down at the table.

"See," he laughed. "I can't resist your mom's cooking! I just have to taste these new muffins!"

Tess took a deep breath. "Grandma and Dad say we'll get used to doing things in a new way. We will, won't we, Mom?"

Mom poured some drinks. "We all will, Tess," she said. "We'll all get used to the changes."

Nathan put his muffin down. "I know one thing that won't change," he said. "We've got the greatest dad and the best mom, and that'll never change!"

Tess nodded. Nathan was right.